NORTH CAROLINA OUTDOORS

100 ADVENTURES FROM MAX PATCH TO MANTEO

Published by *Our State* magazine, Mann Media, Inc.
PO Box 4552, Greensboro, NC 27404
(800) 948-1409 | ourstate.com
Printed in the United States by LSC Communications

EDITOR IN CHIEF: Elizabeth Hudson
EDITORS: Todd Dulaney, Katie Schanze
DESIGN DIRECTOR: Claudia Royston
ART DIRECTOR: Jason Chenier
EDITORIAL DESIGNER: Jeanne King
ASSOCIATE DESIGNER: Hannah Wright
ART ASSISTANT: Kelly Green

Library of Congress Control Number: 2021908323

ON THE COVER:
Max Patch is known as the "crown jewel of the Appalachian Trail." To learn more about this coveted camping spot, turn to page 26.

COVER: NATE BOWERY; BACK COVER: CHRIS HANNANT

NORTH CAROLINA

OUTDOORS

100 ADVENTURES FROM MAX PATCH TO MANTEO

From the Little Pinnacle Overlook, Park Ranger Jesse Anderson keeps close watch on the hawk and raven nesting grounds atop Big Pinnacle. For more on Pilot Mountain, turn to page 34.

PHOTOGRAPH BY ADAM MOWERY

FIRE TOWERS

THEY BROUGHT ALONG a two-foot machete — for bears, you know. Having never spent a night in the woods, Peter Barr and his buddy Brad felt they had to prepare for all possibilities. As overly confident and excessively outfitted college kids, they'd set out from Fontana Dam on a six-day hike along the Appalachian Trail. With each step up Shuckstack Mountain, their 70-pound packs clanked with the gear they'd rented from a military surplus store; their gym sneakers started rubbing blisters. The silent self-recriminations began.

At the summit, they found a good excuse to set down their packs and stretch their toes: There, a tall, rusty Tinkertoy of

The Green Knob Lookout is worth the half-mile hike from the Blue Ridge Parkway. The view from the top provides a panorama of the Black Mountains, as well as the tallest peak in North Carolina, Mount Mitchell.

PHOTOGRAPH BY ANDY TOMS

Fryingpan tower (above) dazzles hikers. Peter Barr's guide to hiking 26 western fire towers includes the restored Mount Cammerer Lookout (opposite) in the Great Smoky Mountains.

a fire tower, known simply as Shuckstack, cast a portentous shadow. Another hiker, having just descended, brushed past Peter and Brad, declaring, "I might be the last one to climb that tower before it falls down."

How could Peter let that stand? He scooted up each wooden, partially rotten step on his rear end, bolts rattling under his shifting weight. Steel beams, blemished by decades of corrosion and graffiti, gave the tower an easy, if unsettling, sway. On one flight, the handrails were missing entirely. At 75 steps, Peter's feet were in the trees, and above that, the physical world seemed to fall away. A few more steps brought him into the cab, where the keeper once watched for fires from an elevation of 4,000 feet.

Wind rolled in and out of the empty

PHOTOGRAPHY BY ANDY TOMS; PORTRAIT BY JACK SOROKIN

window frames in the 7-by-7-foot room. "I looked out at the Southern Appalachians around me, at where we came from near the dam, and out over the range," Peter says. "If I can trace one moment where my life took a new direction, that was it."

In the years following that trip, Peter's fascination with fire towers became an avocation: He studied U.S. Geographical Survey maps to locate the North Carolina lookout sites, and then hiked to find them. About half the time, he discovered that the tower had long since been dismantled or removed. Surviving towers were often in the same sorry shape as Shuckstack. And yet, the astounding vistas these neglected structures revealed seemed to Peter reason enough to protect them.

Now Peter, the trails specialist at Conserving Carolina, spends his spare time drumming up the community support, dollars, and muscle needed for restoration projects like the one completed on Shuckstack in 2014. In the process, many dog-eared, coffee-stained copies of his book, *Hiking North Carolina's Lookout Towers*, have been passed among hikers, particularly those heading up Mount Cammerer or Fryingpan, where what you can see from a fire tower is the whole point.

Which is not to say that the view is all there is to these structures. Like lighthouses, lookouts have outlived their intended purpose, but that's the source of their charm: Relics trip the imagination and spark wonder. — *Louise Jarvis Flynn*

THE BLUE RIDGE MOUNTAINS

WE'RE NOT THE ONLY state that can lay claim to the Appalachian Mountains. We know this. From Georgia to Maine, there are 13 others that can do the same. What some of these other states don't have, though, is the Blue Ridge, a magnificent, mystical segment of the sprawling mountain range.

If you've wondered what gives the Blue Ridge Mountains their distinctive hue, you're not alone. People have done so for centuries. But knowing the science behind this natural phenomenon only makes their appearance more wondrous — even to scientists.

Take Jonathan Horton, a professor of biology at the University of North Carolina at Asheville. Horton holds a doctorate in forestry and specializes in plant physiology.

To understand the color blue, he suggests looking at all of the green. The trees produce "volatile hydrocarbons," or organic hydrogen-carbon compounds.

One such hydrocarbon is isoprene, which is emitted by trees as a way to protect

This is what forever is: endless crests and crowns, all varying shades of soft blue, enveloped by a translucent haze.

PHOTOGRAPH BY WERKSMEDIA/ISTOCK/GETTY IMAGES PLUS

themselves from the stress of excess heat, especially on summer days. After it's released into the air, isoprene interacts with other molecules in the atmosphere, creating the distinctive haze that's made the Blue Ridge Mountains famous.

So why don't *all* mountains appear blue? The answer depends on exactly how much isoprene the trees are producing, Horton says. Isoprene-happy oak trees are plentiful in our neck of the woods, compared with the rest of the Appalachian Mountains. Oaks have been facing decline for years, but western North Carolina remains a stronghold.

"If we get a species shift away from oaks, then our Blue Ridge Mountains might not look as blue," he says.

When it comes to nature, it's not so easy to get a forever guarantee. But we'll continue to surrender our breath to these awe-inspiring blue vistas that are all our own. And we'll count our blessings that we get to live here, a place of such profound beauty.

— *Katie Quine*

Above the French Broad River, at a spot called Lovers' Leap, father-and-daughter hikers Woody and Jennifer Farmer glimpse Hot Springs, where a skillet breakfast awaits at Smokey Mountain Diner.

OPPOSITE: EMILY CHAPLIN; THIS PAGE: TIM ROBISON

HOT SPRINGS

"HIKE YOUR OWN HIKE" – meaning go at your own pace, and if you disapprove of the pace of others, keep it to yourself – is the quasi-official slogan of the Appalachian Trail, and not a bad philosophy of life. It's an approach that Hot Springs residents have taken to heart, in part because they don't have much choice: the AT runs smack through the middle of their town.

Hot Springs, population 650, follows the seasonal rhythms of the trail. What one local merchant calls "harvest time," for instance, happens in the spring. That's when a few thousand northbound hikers pass through.

They eat, rest, resupply, and quickly move on up the trail, leaving plenty of rooms and restaurant tables available for those of us who move at a more leisurely pace. In other words, you can experience Hot Springs like a thru-hiker even if you aren't one. – *Mark Essig*

Boone photographer Tommy White scouts the perfect location to set up his tripod and harness the early-morning energy of Looking Glass Falls near Brevard.

PHOTOGRAPHY BY THOMAS MOORS

LOOKING GLASS FALLS

TOMMY WHITE KNOWS that sometimes, to get the shot, you have to get off the beaten path. He navigates with forceful grace, grabbing on to roots and shimmying backward. A desire to learn the art of waterfall photography is how I end up out in the woods with White. Before sunrise, I'm standing knee-deep in Looking Glass Falls, balancing a DSLR camera on a tripod in rushing water. The creek feels bracing on my skin; the ink-dark forest around us is sleepy and still. White adjusts my lens and frames the shot so that when the dawn rays break over Looking Glass's famous drop, we'll be ready. "The foreground here is so strong that the waterfall becomes a supporting element," White explains. But by the time the sun rises, saturating Looking Glass in gold light as early-bird tourists arrive, he's ready to move on. "It's dead," he pronounces — meaning that beautiful hiking weather is terrible photography weather. We'll have to wait for sunset. — *Morgan Sykes*

13 WATERFALLS FOR ALL

Drive-up Falls

BRIDAL VEIL FALLS

Before the highway was rerouted around this waterfall, you could drive behind it (below). Today, you can still drive up, park, and walk behind it.

U.S. Highway 64
Highlands, NC 28741
(828) 526-2112

SHUNKAWAUKEN FALLS

On the outskirts of Columbus is a 150-foot-tall waterfall that you can see from small pull-offs on both sides.

White Oak Mountain Road
Columbus, NC 28722
(800) 440-7848

SOCO FALLS

This double waterfall in the Qualla Boundary near Cherokee requires a very short walk from U.S. Highway 19.

Blue Ridge Parkway,
Milepost 455.7
Maggie Valley, NC 28751
(800) 334-9036

THIS PAGE: THOMAS MOORS, EMILY CHAPLIN; OPPOSITE: THOMAS MOORS

Kid-friendly

DRY FALLS

Take the kids on the easy, quarter-mile round-trip trail to Dry Falls for a chance to see the world from behind a waterfall.

U.S. Highway 64
Highlands, NC 28741
(828) 524-6441

HIDDEN FALLS

At less than a mile round trip, Indian Creek Trail is one of Hanging Rock State Park's shortest hikes, with picnic tables and restrooms nearby.

Hanging Rock State Park
1005 Visitor Center Drive
Westfield, NC 27053
(336) 593-8480

SKINNY DIP FALLS

Don't fret over the name — the swimming hole at this waterfall is 100 percent family-friendly. And the mile-long round-trip hike is easy.

Blue Ridge Parkway,
Milepost 417
Canton, NC 28716
(828) 348-3400

SLIDING ROCK

This natural water slide (above) dumps into an eight-foot-deep pool. You can participate, or you can watch from an observation area.

7851 Pisgah Highway
Pisgah Forest, NC 28768
(828) 885-7625

About a century ago, a small school sat near Greenland Creek in Jackson County's Panthertown Valley, giving Schoolhouse Falls its name.

Worth the Effort

CATAWBA FALLS

The trail to this series of cascades runs about three miles round trip through lush, mossy forest shaded by 100-foot-tall trees.
3074 Catawba River Road
Old Fort, NC 28762
(828) 652-2144

CRABTREE FALLS

A 2.5-mile loop trail to this waterfall takes hikers through rhododendron thickets. A bridge over the creek in front of the falls offers the best view.
3900 Blue Ridge Parkway
Marion, NC 28752
(828) 668-4282

LINVILLE FALLS

The Plunge Basin Trail from the visitor center leads to an overlook and then down to the bottom of the falls for close-up views.
Blue Ridge Parkway,
Milepost 316
Linville Falls, NC 28647
(828) 348-3400

MINGO FALLS

The quarter-mile hike to the 120-foot-high Mingo Falls is short, but it requires climbing 161 steps.
Mingo Falls Campground
71 Big Cove Road
Cherokee, NC 28719
(865) 436-1200

RAINBOW FALLS

The three-mile round-trip hike from the Grassy Ridge trailhead, near the Gorges State Park parking area, leads to a 150-foot-tall waterfall that's even more spectacular after a rainfall.
976 Grassy Ridge Road
Sapphire, NC 28774
(828) 966-9099

SCHOOLHOUSE FALLS

A 2.5-mile round-trip hike in Nantahala National Forest takes you to small cascades that culminate in an 18-foot freefall. The hike consists of multiple trails, so a Panthertown Valley map is highly recommended.
Panthertown Trailhead
Hogback Spur A
Lake Toxaway, NC 28747
(828) 848-8711

— Mark Kemp

For some of the best rhododendron views in North Carolina, you'll have to hop in the car — and then take a hike!

OPPOSITE: CHARLES HARRIS; THIS PAGE: ANDY TOMS

5 RHODODENDRON ROAD TRIPS

CHIMNEY ROCK STATE PARK

Head down the Great Woodland Adventure Trail or Four Seasons Trail for a stunning display of bright white and pale pink Carolina rhododendron blooms.

742 Chimney Rock Park Road
Chimney Rock, NC 28720

CRAGGY GARDENS

For the best views of hundreds of pink and purple rhododendron blooms, park at the Craggy Gardens Visitor Center and take the gradual uphill hike on the one-mile Craggy Gardens Trail.

Milepost 364
Blue Ridge Parkway

MOUNT JEFFERSON STATE NATURAL AREA

Take a moderately difficult 1.5-mile round-trip hike along the Summit and Rhododendron trails, which, beginning in early June, wind through purple Catawba rhododendron flowers.

1481 Mount Jefferson Road
West Jefferson, NC 28694

WAYAH BALD

For the best opportunity to see native rhododendron — and for a panoramic view of four surrounding states — climb the 53-foot fire tower overlooking Nantahala National Forest, just a short walk from the summit parking lot, in late May or early June.

Forest Service Road 69,
near Franklin

GRANDFATHER MOUNTAIN

You can't go wrong at Grandfather: The vivid pink and purple flowers of Catawba rhododendron frame the trails throughout early to mid-June, and later in the month, the paler pink blooms of Rosebay rhododendron take center stage.

2050 Blowing Rock Highway
Linville, NC 28646

— Katie Schanze

LINVILLE GORGE

JUTTING OUT FROM THE LANDSCAPE like high dives, the jagged cliffs of Hawksbill Mountain rise nearly 2,000 feet above the valley floor, making this summit one of the highest points in Linville Gorge. The roughly one-mile hike to the top starts out gentle before a challenging ascent gives way to a wide, brushy plateau. A trail to the right of a large boulder (you'll know it when you see it) leads to the north side of the mountain, where hikers are rewarded with rare 360-degree views of the gorge and beyond, including Grandfather Mountain, Table Rock, Mount Mitchell, and, on clear days, Charlotte, some 90 miles away. — *Katie King & Andrew Salmon*

Discover incredible views of the gorge from (clockwise) Hawksbill Mountain, Wiseman's View and the Pinnacle.

PHOTOGRAPHY BY EMILY CHA[illegible] HARRIS

Throughout the gorge, climbers can find routes for various skill levels and techniques at (clockwise from this page) The Chimneys, Hawksbill and Shortoff mountains, and Table Rock.

THIS PAGE: DREW MERCER; OPPOSITE: BRYAN MILLER, ERIC CHAMPLIN/ASHEVILLE TRAILS, EMILY CHAPLIN

PHOTOGRAPHY BY JACK SOROKIN

Nature abhors fast drivers. Heintooga Round Bottom Road's speed limit is 15 miles per hour, but rocks and ruts and the occasional stray elk encourage a more leisurely pace.

THE GREAT SMOKY MOUNTAINS

THE APPROACHING WINTER chilled the air, and a hint of yellow dappled the leaves as my husband and I headed down Heintooga Round Bottom Road — a rugged, 14-mile, one-lane road that follows an old rail bed deep into the Smokies. After rounding a few curves, He cut the engine of the car, and the sounds of the forest rushed in — the gurgle of a cascading stream, the cry of a raven, the soughing of wind through woods thick with birch and beech, maple and oak. A sense of timelessness engulfed us.

On either side, trees stretch thick and lush, hiding the forest's secrets. Occasionally, a black bear or elk will venture out. Golden-crowned kinglets, Canada warblers, and other nesting birds fill the branches in spring. Wildflowers cover the ground: purple asters, harebells,

showy bellflowers, jewelweed, bee balm.

And reaching this road-less-traveled is part of the adventure. Turn off the Blue Ridge Parkway at Milepost 458.2, not far from Maggie Valley, and follow a paved two-lane road for about nine miles, until the pavement turns to dirt and gravel. From there, Heintooga Round Bottom Road gradually descends 2,000 feet over 14 miles before ending near the Qualla Boundary, home of the Eastern Band of Cherokee Indians. The park service estimates that each year, about 50,000 people venture down the road, which is open from mid-May until the end of October and is listed on some maps as Balsam Mountain Road.

Even if you don't want to navigate the dirt road, there's a lot to see on the way to it. About three miles after turning off the Blue Ridge Parkway, you'll reach the parking lot for the Masonic Monument at Black Camp Gap, near the entrance to Great Smoky Mountains National Park.

A little farther along is Balsam Mountain Campground, at 5,310 feet the highest campground in the national park system east of the Mississippi.

Half a mile past the campground, the Civilian Conservation Corps built a picnic area in the 1930s as part of its work-relief

PHOTOGRAPHY BY JACK SOROKIN

Heintooga Road runs beside, over, and around Straight Creek on its 14-mile path through the Smokies.

program during the Great Depression.

At the picnic area, the two-lane paved road abruptly ends. A sign warns: "One way only. Narrow, winding unimproved mountain road next 14 miles. No trucks, buses or trailers. ... Driving time 1 hour. Gates locked at dark."

Here, Heintooga Round Bottom Road begins.

We drove partway in on the next-to-last day of the season and saw only one other group: several boys and their father on mountain bicycles, gliding down the gentle grade, followed by their grandfather in a car.

It takes an hour to drive because of the many potholes and bumps, twists and turns. Don't try to take a sports car — you need a good sedan at least.

On the final day of the season we had the road to ourselves, trees towering above, mountain streams tumbling below, the smell of the air fresh and clean. We stopped several times to absorb the quiet beauty. A carpet of ferns. Moss-covered stumps. A trickle of a stream cutting through the dense growth. Surely this is what writer and outdoorsman Horace Kephart had in mind when he described these remote corners of the Smokies as "the back of beyond."

— Elizabeth Leland

Camping atop Max Patch means waking up on a blanket of grasses and ferns, with views of Mount Mitchell to the east and the Great Smoky Mountains to the southwest.

THIS PAGE: ROBERT STEPHENS; OPPOSITE: NATE BOWERY

MAX PATCH

BY THE TIME northbound thru-hikers on the Appalachian Trail reach Madison County, they've traveled more than 200 miles from their starting point in Georgia on their way to Maine. They've covered much of that distance in deep forest, becoming intimately familiar with the bark of poplar trees and the sound of streams. They've been sheltered by wilderness, and the grandeur of their long journey has been intangible — until the forest opens to reveal Max Patch, a Southern Appalachian bald in Pisgah National Forest.

Suddenly, they are taller than the trees, standing on a 350-acre tract of land with an unimpeded view of their surroundings. From 4,600 feet above sea level, they can see the magnitude of their undertaking: the wild land they've traveled, the peaks they have yet to mount — all of it extraordinary.

The glory of this moment has given the bald a reputation as the "crown jewel of the Appalachian Trail." — *Leigh Ann Henion*

After a day on the trails, hikers and bikers gather outside Pisgah Tavern, part of Sam and Jordan Salman's bike shop, for a local brew.

PISGAH FOREST

FOOD TRUCKS and mountain bikes flank the entrance of The Hub bike shop in Brevard. Inside, mechanics with bushy beards twist wrenches while packs of mountain bikers sip craft brews and recount what sounds like the best day ever. But underneath The Hub's hip surface is a family business with a passion for Pisgah Forest. "We put a lot of emphasis on making a place for people to come hang out," owner Sam Salman says. Ten years ago, when he and his wife, Jordan, bought a small bike shop in Brevard, there weren't many places like theirs serving beer. It was actually skiers, rather than cyclists, who inspired Sam's vision for The Hub. He wanted to re-create the lodge scene known as après ski, but with a mountain biker's bent. "There was no post-adventure community," Sam says. "It became apparent that Pisgah needed an après scene." In 2015, the Salmans purchased an empty lot across the street from their initial location. Their new real estate put them right at the entrance to Pisgah Forest, and The Hub essentially became the new trailhead for some of the best mountain biking on the East Coast. And while the Salmans' bike shop/tavern is all about having a good time, The Hub has also embraced its responsibilities as a steward of the forest: The shop donates $5 from every bike rental to the Pisgah Conservancy and helps maintain a number of trails. "I see The Hub as the direction this community wants to move," Sam says. "They're all coming together because they love Pisgah."

— *Phil Morgan*

THE HUB
11 Mama's Place, Pisgah Forest, NC 28768
(828) 884-8670, thehubpisgah.com

OPPOSITE: TOMMY PENICK; THIS PAGE: JACK SOROKIN

At Southern Highlands Reserve, we find the very best of what humans and nature can create together, honoring the legacy of the land and preserving its beauty forever.

PHOTOGRAPH BY THOMAS MOORS

SOUTHERN HIGHLANDS RESERVE

HIGH ON TOXAWAY MOUNTAIN, Robert and Betty Balentine bought a lot — and were stunned by what they found: It was lush and beautiful, to be sure, but a survey of the land showed that it was also home to diverse plant communities and rare species. They knew they had to preserve it. Now, 120 acres — once slated for development — are under a conservation easement, and a staff of horticulturists and naturalists research, catalog, share, and care for this slice of the Southern Appalachian landscape. One of the state's best-kept secrets, Southern Highlands Reserve is a native plant arboretum, a research center, a living laboratory. Most of all, it's a place of unparalleled beauty.

— *Katie Saintsing*

558 Summit Ridge Road, Lake Toxaway, NC 28747
(828) 885-2050, southernhighlandsreserve.org

GRANDFATHER MOUNTAIN

I CLIMBED FOR 15 MINUTES before trying a cast. Here, in the steep country below Grandfather Mountain, creeks pour off the land in great stair steps of falling water. I didn't even know the name of the stream. It was wild and twisty and kinked up like a branch of rhododendron, white as granite, thick as mountain fog. In this part of the High Country, you can jump across creeks in a single bound, except for the pools, which can be 20 feet wide. They might be two feet deep or 10. In a mountain stream, a trout stream, the pools are where the magic lies.

I cast the fly, once, twice, three times. Nothing. The fourth cast, however, was gold. The fish hit and sounded, ran for the darkest chamber, then fought all the way to the throat of the riffle where I crouched behind a fallen log. It was a brown trout, a little less than a foot long, its flanks peppered with orange and black spots. In the corner of its jaw was a bright yellow fly — a Yaller Hammer — a pattern whose history and heritage bind it close to North Carolina trout streams. In fact, that fly was the inspiration for that morning's quest.

The Yaller Hammer is a traditional Southern Appalachian fly pattern, so old that no one is quite sure when it first appeared. I'd never fished with the fly until I climbed that creek with a singular purpose: to catch a trout on the historic pattern.

I slipped the hook from the fish's jaw, and held the trout in the water's flow. It dashed from my loose grip, a streak of copper lightning. Then I climbed, plumbing each pool, fishing toward Grandfather Mountain.

— T. Edward Nickens

PHOTOGRAPHY BY ANDREW KORNYLAK

Even with surefire flies, you don't just plop your line in a stream. There's a proper way to stalk a trout.

PILOT MOUNTAIN STATE PARK

TECHNICALLY, IT'S NOT EVEN A mountain. Pilot Mountain — and the entire Sauratown range — didn't burst from the ground due to tectonic shifts or volcanic activity. Rather, these distinctive elevations remained after the land around them eroded over time. In fact, the peaks we see today were once at the bottom of a shallow sea. They're merely sand transformed by heat and pressure into sturdy quartzite. Over time, the quartzite broke off, forming cliffs and creating the iconic knob known as Big Pinnacle.

A destination for generations of school field trips, hikes, and family picnics, the mountain gained worldwide fame — and a stream of new visitors — when Andy Griffith

PHOTOGRAPH BY MICHAEL STEED

From the Little Pinnacle Overlook at Pilot Mountain State Park, the iconic Big Pinnacle appears to glow in the dawn light.

At Pilot Knob Inn (opposite), guests can stay in one of the six cabins, which are renovated century-old tobacco barns, or the inn's five suites.

made it Mayberry's notable landmark, too. While the land is now a state park, before that and for much longer, it was a local tourist attraction and often the site of a rollicking party scene.

"THAT PEAK OVER THERE," SAYS KATHY Hunter, pointing toward Big Pinnacle, which is now closed to the public, "they used to have wooden steps that went up the side of it." Hunter works by the entrance to the park, at Pilot Knob Inn. She remembers exploring the mountain around the time it became a state park in 1968 and just before the steps — which led up the vertical, 200-foot-high knob that caps the 2,200 feet of elevation — were removed. The wooden stairs were built by W.L. Spoon, an engineer who purchased the mountain in the 1920s and developed it for tourism. "He approached the mountain as a kind of P.T. Barnum character," explains Mark Farnsworth, a Pilot Mountain historian. "He was a showman and promoter."

But Spoon wasn't the mountain's first booster. In the middle of the 19th century, members of the Gilliam family owned Pilot Mountain, along with a hotel at its base, which they publicized nationally. "People wanted to see this curiosity of nature, a mountain that stands alone," Farnsworth says.

During World War II, a local Chevrolet dealer, J.W. Beasley, bought the property and turned it into a local hangout to see and be seen. To draw crowds and charge admission, Beasley built a swimming pool and a dance-hall pavilion, where campgrounds are now.

The pool stayed open until Beasley's widow, Pearl, sold the property to the state for a park. While folks would miss the pool parties and bands, locals were grateful that the family didn't sell the mountain for private development. Today, the wild nights may be over, but the quiet, starry skies over Pilot Mountain are just as magical.

— Jane Borden

OPPOSITE: MICHAEL STEED; THIS PAGE: ADAM MOWERY

The Bullhole's dam was built in 1900 by the Erwin Cotton Mill. Today, it provides a beautiful backdrop to splashing summer fun.

PHOTOGRAPHY BY REVIVAL CREATIVES

COOLEEMEE FALLS

WHERE THE YADKIN RIVER tumbles over Cooleemee Falls between Davie and Rowan counties, a cool escape from the summer sun awaits. Kids slide down slick rock surfaces on bare legs or inner tubes while adults dangle their feet in the chilly water. And vice versa. Because here, anyone can be a kid. Known as The Bullhole (legend has it that, years ago, a bull ox hauling timber across the river slipped near the falls and disappeared into a whirlpool), this popular summer hangout was once the site of one of Rowan County's largest gristmills, as well as many late 19th-century Masonic picnics. The area's significance as a gathering place inspired local leaders to create a 30-acre "RiverPark," including The Bullhole, which officially opened in 2004. Today, up to 250 visitors come to this spot each day to swim, fish, sunbathe, and slide. Stand under the falls for a pounding massage; take a freezing dip in one of the deep swimming holes; bury your friends in the sand on the beach, deposited on the riverbank by a flood. Because here, anyone can be a kid. — *Katie King*

645 Erwin Temple Church Road, Woodleaf, NC 27054
(336) 284-6040, cooleemee.org

David Craft, chair of the Uwharrie Trailblazers since 2015, first hiked the length of the trail in 1978 as a 15-year-old Boy Scout. Today, he ensures that it's well maintained for a new generation of hikers.

PHOTOGRAPHY BY ADAM MOWERY

UWHARRIE TRAIL

JOEY MOFFITT WORE A T-SHIRT, boots, and faded blue jeans with frayed hems. His hair was brown, longish, and scraggly. I was still in high school; Joey was a couple years older. It was the late 1970s, and he had a little orange Jensen-Healey convertible that we would take for spins along the rolling country roads that cut through the northern part of Uwharrie National Forest just south of Asheboro. During those drives, we'd talk about everything under the sun over the din of a cassette tape blaring Southern rock music by Lynyrd Skynyrd or the Allman Brothers Band. On this day, we were talking about hiking and camping and canoeing.

"My father wrote a book about these woods," Joey shouted over the music as we rounded a curve on Pisgah Covered Bridge Road, the wind whipping our hair into knotted string mops. Later, at his house, Joey pulled out a dog-eared, 152-page, stapled-together hodgepodge of frontier

David Craft (left) spends up to 40 hours a month with the Uwharrie Trailblazers, whacking weeds, picking up trash, and maintaining the integrity of the trails.

folklore entitled *An Afternoon Hike Into the Past*. Inside the booklet, in plain Courier typeface, Troop 570 Scoutmaster Joseph T. Moffitt described his childhood in the Uwharries of the 1920s and '30s; told stories of spirits that haunted these hills, of moonshiners and abandoned gold mines; and shared old-time recipes, herbal remedies, and lessons on trapping, basketmaking, and surviving in the wilderness. At the back of the book were a few pages of maps — hand-drawn by Joey for an Eagle Scout project — of the Uwharrie Trail.

In 1968, the elder Moffitt spearheaded one of the earliest outdoor recreation projects that the 51,000-acre Uwharrie National Forest had seen since its federal designation seven years before. Moffitt, his Scout troop, and other Asheboro-area outdoor enthusiasts began cutting the first 30 miles of what he envisioned as a 50-mile path from the Birkhead Mountains in Randolph County into the wilds of Montgomery County to the south. Most hikers were familiar with the 300-plus miles of Appalachian Trail that thread through western North Carolina and eastern Tennessee. Moffitt's idea: create a *mini* Appalachian Trail right smack in the heart of the state. The problem was, the Randolph County stretch of federally owned land looked like pieces of an unfinished jigsaw puzzle amid mostly privately owned property. Cutting a trail straight through to Montgomery would be tricky. Since Moffitt

Hikers Michael Smith (left) and Gifford Del Grande used hiking sticks to navigate a dry Walkers Creek during the 2019 Uwharrie Trail Thru-Hike.

had grown up in the area and knew many of the landowners, he made handshake deals with some of them to connect the northern part with the southern part just below a spot called Jumping Off Rock.

By the early '70s, U.S. Forest Service District Ranger Robert Carey and members of the Youth Conservation Corps had completed a more official 20-mile Montgomery County stretch of the Uwharrie Trail, which today begins at Jumping Off Rock and runs south to NC Highway 24/27 near the community of Woodrun. But the northern trail system in Randolph County remained fragmented, as some of the landowners changed their minds about allowing hikers through their property, and other privately owned tracts changed hands over the years. By 1980, progress had stalled on Moffitt's idea of a full, 50-mile Uwharrie Trail. To the U.S. Forest Service, those old handshake deals that he'd made were never binding anyway. And until all gaps in the Randolph County part of the trail were sewn up — owned and recognized by the Forest Service — Moffitt's ultimate vision would not be realized.

This is where the Uwharrie Trailblazers come in. Officially formed in 2012, the ragtag group of longtime outdoor swashbucklers had been gathering in the forest since the late '90s to continue the efforts that Moffitt began: blazing trails, constructing new ones, and helping maintain sanctioned parts of the current trail and its side paths. Because the Uwharrie Trail won't never be finished. It's always got to be maintained.

— Mark Kemp

OPPOSITE: JON BLACK, ADAM MOWERY; THIS PAGE: JON BLACK

The "Mall Rated" sticker is a joking play on the more serious "Trail Rated" badges, and an ironic retort to the insult, "Your vehicle is only good for shopping." Clearly, this mud-spattering Jeep Cherokee is not headed to the mall. And neither is Ken Piedrahita (opposite), who calmly navigates a jagged incline in his Land Rover.

PHOTOGRAPHY BY ANDREW KORNYLAK

UWHARRIE MOUNTAINS

TOMMY GRAY STANDS AT THE TOP of Scrambler Hill, having just mastered a precarious challenge. Minutes before, he'd maneuvered up the steep, rocky climb in his Jeep Wrangler JKU, and now he's looking down on a fellow driver who's having less luck. A Toyota FJ Cruiser has surrendered to the hill. If the driver makes the wrong move, the Cruiser could flip.

Gray rests his hands on his hips and cocks his head. "Bit of a pickle," he says.

Come across this scene anywhere else, and you'd see flashing lights and first responders. Come across it during a weekend of off-roading in the Uwharrie Mountains, and the most alarm you'll hear is from Gray, who casually understates the predicament. Even the Cruiser's driver and his passenger seem more curious than concerned.

It's hard to pity this group for getting into such messes. After all, the 15 drivers and their passengers signed up for this. They drove to the Uwharries to take their vehicles onto forest trails that thread narrowly between trees, and to traverse boulders and hills that seem more like obstructions than obstacles. It's also hard to pity a group that's having so much fun, even in a pickle. In fact, figuring out how to *un*pickle a situation seems to be the point.

Ahead, there's always something: a rock scramble, a steep hill, trees. *How wide is that opening? How much clearance is underneath?* Uwharries off-roading isn't so

much for daredevils as it is for tacticians; it's three-dimensional Tetris with thousands of dollars at stake.

More than that, it's a hell of a ride.

THINK OF OFF-ROADING, AND YOU'LL LIKELY conjure images of a Jeep commercial. That's the problem. That style of driving hurts the land and contributes to erosion, something the Uwharries are no strangers to. They're among the oldest mountains in North America, once ancient volcanic peaks rising 20,000 feet. But river erosion wore down those peaks, and now they rise only about 1,000 feet at their tallest — just enough to make this landscape of rivers, lakes, and trails an off-roading playground.

The thing is, the Uwharries also hold sacred land filled with the history of the Catawba tribe. Most off-roading groups understand their legal and ethical responsibility to protect the land. In fact, those groups have become partners with the Forest Service in its conservation efforts. The drivers on today's ride are among those partners. The ride is affiliated with the larger American Adventurist Appalachian Rendezvous, a weekend event that invites enthusiasts to kayak, mountain bike, and off-road in ways that respect the land.

More than the thrill and more than the challenge, off-roaders say they seek an escape. They find camaraderie in connecting with their fellow outdoor enthusiasts who flee sterile offices for a rock scramble in the mountains. — *Jen Tota McGivney*

PHOTOGRAPHY BY ANDREW KORNYLAK

Drivers share their experience with others during four-wheeling events. On Perimeter Hill, a long and hazardous climb, a driver gets pointers on negotiating the challenge.

THIS PAGE: ALAN GARVICK; OPPOSITE: HEATHER SCHAEFGEN-RUSSELL

JORDAN LAKE STATE RECREATION AREA

SINCE 1782, the bald eagle has been our national bird. Yet by the mid-1960s, it was almost extinct in the lower 48 states, with fewer than 500 nesting pairs remaining. Although an avid outdoorsman, I went many years without seeing a single bald eagle in North Carolina or neighboring states. By the early 1980s, there were no nesting eagles here. It seems almost inconceivable that this symbol of strength and freedom was almost lost to illegal hunting and the indiscriminate use of pesticides, including DDT. Fortunately, the bald eagle is one of the great success stories of the conservation movement. You can now see them soaring over lakes and larger rivers statewide — including Jordan Lake, home to the largest concentration in the eastern U.S. The bird is a defining symbol of effective management, legislation, and messaging. — *Tom Earnhardt*

After narrowly avoiding extinction, bald eagles have made a comeback. They soar over Jordan Lake (opposite) in Chatham County.

EASTERN

SAND DUNES OF THE OUTER BANKS

WHEN I WAS A BOY, my cousins and I used to leave our family's Kitty Hawk seaside cottage after lunch and tromp away from the ocean, walking west toward the soundside woods.

Most afternoons, we stopped just shy of the woods line at a single, large, teapot-shaped dune absolutely swarming, in summertime, with briars and trumpet vine and scuppernongs. We found what small bit of shade this dune afforded, took our fill of grapes, and stared back to our small, white, red-roofed cottage silhouetted against the deep blue sea.

In time, I found and strode other ranges of North Carolina sands: One, of course, was the great sand mountain called Jockey's Ridge, just down the road apiece. I once climbed it as a boy with my father on a day when the wind was really blowing and the sand was stinging my legs — it hurt, and I was crying, till he picked me up and sang me

PHOTOGRAPH BY CHRIS HANNANT

a song, carrying me the rest of the way to the top. There were the dunes of Shackleford Banks and, farther south, of Sunset Beach and Bird Island, where the Kindred Spirit mailbox, full of its soul-baring notebooks, stood atilt among the sea oats in all weather. And, too, the beach and steep live-oak dune bluff of Durant Island looking north across Albemarle Sound; the many miles of low dunes out on Core Banks; the East Beach on Bald Head Island, up where Corn Cake Inlet once was; and the half-mile walk from marshes to sea on Bear Island through its own teapot dunes.

My wife, Ann, and I have lately taken to what, on Ocracoke, passes for a mountain range: the piney woods and live oaks of the Hammock Hills, not far northeast of

Jockey's Ridge formed 3,000 to 4,000 years ago. Only its six-inch top layer is dry sand; the wet sand beneath helps maintain the dune system's shape.

the village. Even higher and larger are the great forested dune ridges of the 1,000-acre Buxton Woods, lying between NC Highway 12 and the national seashore, just west of Cape Hatteras.

Yet, after a lifetime of striding and shuffling and threading my way about all of these places and many more — up, over, and through the lovely and constantly changing sand masses of our coast — I must own up and play a favorite, hard as it is to do so, and admit my deep, abiding love of Run Hill.

IN 1987, I FOUND MYSELF YET AGAIN ON THE Outer Banks, at Nags Head beach. Ann and I, new to each other, met up there and drove south, over the old Bonner Bridge at Oregon Inlet to Pea Island, found a pull-off that would not sink our borrowed sports car in the sand, and walked over the dune to swim in the cool Atlantic.

Across Highway 12, we walked slowly down the long, curving sand levee beside one of the big waterfowl impoundments, stilts and herons and egrets all around us, and mullet jumping, too. I climbed atop an earthwork and stared north. Ann clambered up after me, and we stood together as the brilliant late-afternoon sun's long light lay over the tall, golden grasses.

Two trails snake through the 426-acre Jockey's Ridge State Park — one runs from the parking lot to the ridge and on over to Roanoke Sound; the other makes a loop through wetlands and maritime thickets near the sound.

The next morning, Ann and I took a much longer stroll down the lanes of the Nature Conservancy's Nags Head Woods. She had helped put this treasured preserve together, and she wanted to show me places that she had come to love back in the woods: the small, old family cemeteries with chalk-white marble grave slabs, conch shells atop them that marked recent visits of kin. She wanted me to see the steep sand slopes forested with pines and live oaks; the small, dark ponds at the bottoms of the hills. And lastly, a very long, slow-rising path ending abruptly — surprisingly — in the 20-foot-tall face of a vast, living, moving dune, a sand mountain rivaling the more southerly Jockey's Ridge in size: Run Hill.

The next high dune to the north was Kill Devil Hill, where the Wright brothers first flew, yet it was the view west from the summit of Run Hill that truly caught me. I found it simply stunning, first looking down from above the treetops into the steadily sanding forest, next over the broad salt marshes below and the great cove those marshes lined, and, at last, across the long reach of Roanoke Sound toward Manteo.

"What's the cove right down there called?" I asked Ann. Smiling, she gazed out upon it for a few seconds, then said exuberantly: "Breathtaking Bay."

Years later, I learned she had made up that name right on the spot.

And just for me. — *Bland Simpson*

PHOTOGRAPH BY CHRIS HANNANT

The pristine South Core Banks, known to anglers as Davis Island, transforms into a campground during the fall and spring drum runs. Surf fishermen arrive in one-of-a-kind campers for the catch of a lifetime.

PHOTOGRAPHY BY BAXTER MILLER

SOUTH CORE BANKS

THEY COME RIDING ACROSS the sand like cowboys, rising and falling like the waves on the shore, pickup trucks rigged up with campers on their backs, extended racks jutting from the front and rear loaded down with coolers and surf rods and generators. They ride with the kind of courage you only really find here, on the edge of North Carolina's wildest shore: South Core Banks, known to many as Davis Island.

Ten miles from Cape Lookout Lighthouse might as well be a million miles from home, as wind from a nor'easter blasts the entire length of the barrier island. Yet the anglers are still reading the water, driving up and down the shoreline in homemade vehicles, looking for cuts and sloughs, points and drops, looking for a place to park, to "drop anchor" and settle in for a long and stormy night. The drum are running, and in this state, that means an old-school reunion of the old-school camper-fishermen who call this island home.

"Home away from home," Stan Bassinger says. He's a grizzled, wind-burned angler from Salisbury on a four-day survival trip

“When you’re standing on the beach, fishing, everybody’s equal.”

with his friend Charlie Hutton. They’ve been coming here for more than 30 years, drawn by one of the last original seascapes in this part of the country, a land that changes constantly, yet looks much as it must have hundreds of years ago.

That’s what draws these intrepid fishermen to the last of our wild shores to test themselves against the elements. This is no place for the meek. The virtually uninhabited sliver of an island is a destination for some of the quirkiest adventurers you will ever meet.

THESE ARE SOME OF THE BEST SURF anglers on earth. Some are in tents. Some stay in the rustic cabins built just for fishermen. But the most dedicated are those who camp in their own contraptions, the same vehicles that brought them here: modified off-road mechanical marvels. Some are new and some are no more than rusted old RVs and trailers, vans and school buses — four-wheel experiments equipped with refrigerators and shortwave radios and bunk beds and stoves and kitchen tables covered in hooks and leaders and weights and fish guts.

Lance Brown, the president of the Davis Island Fishing Foundation, has been coming here most of his life to fish for prize-size red drum. “It’s important to understand that these people aren’t irresponsible,” Brown says of the camper-fishermen. “These vehicles aren’t junk. These are built for a purpose, and that’s to fish on South Core Banks.”

The vehicles line up on the beach,

On Davis Island, empty rod holsters mean the owner's gone fishing. As for the stiletto chair (opposite), for one group of fishing buddies, the lucky soul who catches the most fish gets the "honor" of fishing from the chair the next year.

positioned just above the high-water mark, like a flea market on the edge of reality. Fishing rods are mounted in crude holders or planted in the sand or built into the vehicles themselves, like snaggled teeth tethered to the ocean by miles and miles of fishing line.

"This is serious business," Bassinger says.

The sky behind him has turned deep black, and the wind is rocking his truck camper. Up and down the beach, fishermen are still casting into the churning waters. Yes, a nor'easter is blowing in, and this is going to be a long night on the island.

But the drum are still running. The men stand side by side, telling stories and daring the wind and the rain to end a trip they've been planning all year.

"When you're standing on the beach, fishing, everybody's equal," Brown says. "Everybody here is here for the same reason." To catch a fish you can't even keep.

Anglers are in search of red drum that have grown to "citation" length. The little puppy drum that land on your hook, well, those you can keep. They provide entertainment or dinner. But the minimum 40-inch red drum is the one that the North Carolina Marine Fisheries Division will award you a certificate of citation for landing. It's the elusive catch that makes everything about this island worth the effort. And the effort can be exhausting.

When morning light finally comes, the drum are gone, blown away, and a line of campers waits for the ferry. The anglers appear as worn out as their vehicles. Looking back from the middle of Core Sound, the barrier island shrinks in the distance as they head toward a good night's sleep. And maybe a trip to the auto parts store. *— Ed Hardin*

PHOTOGRAPHY BY BAXTER MILLER

A former owner of this land, Sam Jones, chose to be buried here with his beloved horse Ikey D, among ancient live oaks twisting their knobby arms toward the sun.

PHOTOGRAPHY BY EMILY CHAPLIN & CHRIS COUNCIL

SPRINGER'S POINT

THE TREES AT SPRINGER'S POINT on Ocracoke Island huddle together for protection against battering storms; within that dome of maritime forest, plants and wildlife flourish. A previous owner of the land, Sam Jones, chose not to develop it, recognizing that he could not improve upon its natural beauty. Today, the Coastal Land Trust ensures that what is now the 122-acre Springer's Point Nature Preserve remains untouched and open to the public. From the shore, kayaks and sailboats floating on Pamlico Sound echo seafaring vessels of the past: Centuries ago, Native Americans and colonial pilots found refuge here. In the 1700s, the pirate Edward Teach (aka Blackbeard) often visited from his home across the sound in Bath — and fought his final battle on nearby waters, known to this day as Teach's Hole. Now, those who find the near-secret entrance to the preserve — tucked in a neighborhood on Loop Road — follow a sandy path through silvery maritime trees and down to the beach, walking in the footsteps of ponies and pirates. — *Katie Saintsing*

Waves, like this emerald barrel, offer an enviable ride for the fewer than 300 residents who call Rodanthe home.

RODANTHE

EVERYTHING IS ALIVE and everything changes. In Rodanthe, this is not an abstract idea but an undeniable and deeply felt reality. Just look to Highway 12: The ocean is reclaiming this road built on sand, which is frequently closed due to high winds, storm surges, and reconstruction. On one side of the road: swaying marsh grasses and a rippling sound-side pond. On the other: waves breaking onto a beach. Clouds tumble overhead, and a whipping wind bends the sea oats. No day for sunbathers, but surfers are out in force.

There are people who surf — and then there are *surfers*, like those who live here. To settle in Rodanthe is to commit to a different kind of life, one that requires sacrifices and accommodations to this narrow sliver of land. The tourist season is shorter and the hurricane season is longer, but the beauty is more breathtaking, too.

When waves are breaking, surfers in Rodanthe cancel other plans — or show up late with wet hair and irrepressible grins. Spend time with them, and you'll sense something unusual, something you don't encounter often. At first, it's hard to name, and then you realize what it is: their quiet, pure joy. — *Krista Bremer*

OPPOSITE: CHRIS HANNANT; THIS PAGE: MATT LUSK

BEAR ISLAND

DARRYL MARSH IS ONE for quieter seasons. In the hectic summer, he loads his skiff with vacationers at Dudley's Marina in Cedar Point and pilots them through the winding backwaters, past the Hammocks Beach landing, and over to Bear Island. There, locals and tourists from many states away compete with each other to find shells. The bounty is there, but it is spread among many.

Winter's brisk temperatures and blustery winds may slow business, but Darryl knows that the off-season opens another door: to sand dollars. Lots and lots of sand dollars. Because when the tide is out and competition is low, more treasures may be found by those who know where — and when — to look. "You've got to be willing to be cold and wear lined boots," he says as he prepares to pilot its low *putt putt putt*, and, with a satisfied thump, Buxton lies down at our feet. We clear the no-wake zone, Darryl throttles up, and the breeze turns into a welcome wind that beats at our skin,

Capt. Darryl Marsh and his furry first mate, Buxton, try their shelling luck around the shoals of Hammocks Beach State Park in Onslow County.

MATT RAY PHOTOGRAPHY

clearing away the funky smell of the marsh grass and replacing it with brisk salt air that feels primal, even ancestral.

We pass by Browns Island, and Darryl points to a sandbar on the Bear Island side, just revealed by the tide. "Nice and low," he says of the water. "And there's no one else out here. That's a good thing."

Buxton goes to the bow; he knows what's coming. As soon as Darryl slows the throttle and gives the dog the go-ahead, Buxton leaps from the boat into barely a foot of water, stirring up the sand into watery clouds that mask what might be below. Darryl laughs and shakes his head. "You're not making it easy, Buxton," he says.

As we splash through calf-deep water, eyes focused on sand, Darryl explains the serendipitous nature of shell seeking. While it's important to hit the right spots when the tide is low, there's no predicting what you'll find. The capricious nature of the pursuit is part of its magic. The water laps at my feet, and I keep searching. — *Cate Doty*

Sand dollars, Scotch bonnets, and whelks are plentiful in winter, when Captain Darryl's guests have many of the sandbars around Bear Island all to themselves. (The Bear Island ferry doesn't run January to March.)

MATT RAY PHOTOGRAPHY

SHACKLEFORD BANKS

THERE ARE NO AMENITIES on Shackleford Banks, where I went to see the horses. That's how I wanted it; I was eager for wild. This slim barrier island, part of Cape Lookout National Seashore, delivered, for it is as untamed as the 100-plus horses that live there. From its windswept shore, reachable only by boat, I could still see the foggy townscapes of Morehead City and Beaufort, and the nearby Cape Lookout lighthouse, but otherwise, I'd left the world behind. Nine miles long, less than a mile wide, the island is mostly flat, although small dunes and thick shrubs and live oaks growing along the northern sound side provide patches of shelter. The

By law, the number of wild horses on Shackleford Banks ranges from 120 to 130, which is considered the ideal number for a healthy herd.

PHOTOGRAPH BY CHARLES HARRIS

horses survive entirely on marsh grass and sea oats. They find freshwater ponds or dig holes in the sand and wait for them to fill. Descendants of horses abandoned by Spaniards and other colonists as early as the 1500s, they are a rugged and resilient breed, kin to other Outer Banks herds found near Corolla, Ocracoke, and in the Rachel Carson Reserve. As a guide led my group toward the herd, the clouds exploded with rain, and spectacular lightning whipped and sizzled down from the sky. We ran back to the ferry. Safely aboard, I glimpsed the faraway herd, majestic in their vulnerability, calmly grazing as the elements crashed around them. — *Marianne Gingher*

MOUNTAINS-TO-SEA TRAIL

BOB HILLYER'S SUV HAS A Mountains-to-Sea Trail vanity plate on the back. Inside, it smells like Off! Deep Woods. When he gets out, he and his companion, Dr. Bill Blackley, slather themselves in bug spray.

The trail, at this point, does not exist here. Hillyer and Blackley follow its future path, starting at Preacher Field Road, just inside the Wilkes County line west of Elkin. Behind a winery are a few lonely graves under a tall walnut tree. One belongs to a man who was George Washington's bodyguard. "Gonna highlight that when the trail runs through here," Hillyer says. Then,

Some of the Mountain-to-Sea Trail's most strenuous spots are in the west, including this stretch through the Linville Gorge.

PHOTOGRAPH BY JUSTIN COSTNER

they walk into the woods toward Big Elkin Creek. Hillyer has a roll of orange tape, and every so often, he'll tie a bit of it to a tree, the knot facing the side where the trail will run. On gentle slopes with a grade of 5 percent or less, the trail can go pretty much where you need it to. If it's steeper, it might need to zigzag or undulate over the terrain so that heavy rains don't wash it out. On the steepest parts, you need a switchback.

The Mountains-to-Sea Trail is 1,175 miles long. It runs from Clingmans Dome on the Tennessee border all the way to Jockey's Ridge State Park on the Outer Banks, ending on top of whatever sand dune happens to be the tallest that day. The path in the western part of the state is almost exclusively trail, running across mountains and through forests on public land, winding over and around peaks until it reaches Stone Mountain State Park, 300 miles from the trailhead.

Then, things get complicated.

From there, the MST follows a lot of roads. It runs through towns, over sidewalks, back into woods, and then down asphalt shoulders, weaving its way along lakeshores north of Greensboro, on a riverwalk next to the Eno River in Hillsborough, along greenways around Durham and Raleigh, and down toward the Neuse River. From there, it dips into the Sandhills, across the fall line into the Coastal Plain, and up toward Cedar Island. The last 81 miles or so are a combination of ferry rides, bridge crossings, and walks along the white, sloped beaches of the Outer Banks.

The MST follows trails in the west and roads in the east for a simple reason: It is exponentially easier to run a new trail across public land than it is to convince someone to let you build a trail across their private property. The largest swaths of national forest, parkland, and other public lands are in the west. Putting the trail in there was the easy part.

The nonprofit Friends of the Mountains-to-Sea Trail is helping take care of the hard part. They help plan and maintain the trail by organizing loosely affiliated groups of trail lovers in counties across the state. The trail is part of the state parks system, but it's maintained by a patchwork of local governments and volunteers. So the path appears a few feet at a time, wherever it can, thanks to the generosity of people who don't mind

As it heads eastward, North Carolina's longest trail runs through Roseboro before following 19 miles of forest road through stands of longleaf pine and pocosins in Pender County (opposite).

OPPOSITE: JOEY SEAWELL; THIS PAGE: CHARLES HARRIS

a few hikers crossing their land to attain a bigger goal.

So when people ask Hillyer when the trail will be completed, he answers: It is complete. We're just changing it, bit by bit, to get it off the roads. That, too, is the answer that Friends of the MST gives to the question it gets the most. "I say it's done," says Kate Dixon, the organization's executive director. "We're just making it better."

At any given time, there are several dozen communities across the state that are in some stage of trail development, trying to organize engineering plans, easement paperwork, and crews of volunteer trail builders and maintainers.

All of it requires plenty of know-how, orange tape, and frequent walks through the woods. On the way back up the hill, Hillyer eyes one of the flags that he left tied to a small hickory tree. He furrows his brow, unties the ribbon, and attaches it to another tree. It's a better route, he says. Then, he pulls down a vine. He adjusts his feet. Waits for a bit. It takes time to create a new way forward. — *Jeremy Markovich*

SCENIC RIVERS

TRICKLE TO TORRENT, down mountainsides and through valleys, North Carolina's rivers braid our state, plait our places together. Without rivers — our vast and interconnecting network of free-flowing waters to the sounds and sea, to lakes and reservoirs — we'd be lost.

The Tar, the Eno, the Dan. We are bound to them and bound by them.

Before the first rutted road, there were rivers. They guided settlers, became outposts, determined where our towns would be. Rivers were our earliest landmarks.

The Neuse, the Deep, the Tuckasegee. They claim us from our first toddling footsteps into a current, wading into the wet, the feel of water flowing beneath an instep, around a shin, up a goose-pimpled forearm. They own us from that first teeter on a moss-slippery rock, that first cautious lifting of a stone to glimpse a scuttling salamander or crawfish. A few years later, they laugh with us as we try, with sticks and stones, to dam them. Later still, they capture us with that first cast into a shaded pool, that first dip of a paddle or ski or inner-tube float. They cool our foreheads and our sodas and our Chardonnay; they douse our campfires and fill our canteens and sing us to sleep.

The Brunswick, the Mayo, the North Toe. Before there were swimming pools shocked clean with chlorine, there were swimming holes made by rivers. Before carved fonts in churches, local rivers stood in for the River Jordan at baptisms, when the sins of the world washed away like a floating feather.

As it winds through northeastern North Carolina, the Roanoke moves more water than any other river in the state.

The Pee Dee, the Pamlico, the Roanoke. What fisherman, what canoer, what waterfall chaser, what hiker, hasn't believed himself the first to discover a secret, shaded fishing spot, an unnavigable chute, a frothing cascade, a secluded swimming hole? Our rivers are narrow enough to wade across in mere steps, and wide enough to sail over in elegant, masted ships.

The Smith, the Scuppernong, the Swannanoa, and so many miles of others. Forever may they flow.

— *Susan Stafford Kelly*

8 STOPS FOR HUNGRY HIKERS

The Whiteside Burger at Whiteside Brewing Co. in Cashiers will satisfy even the biggest appetites. At Uwharrie Mercantile in Troy (opposite), coffee and sandwiches make for a delicious post-hike lunch.

Asheville

BLACK DOME MOUNTAIN SPORTS

This local outfitter has been gearing up hikers since 1984, and the addition of a bar, Conspiracy, has made it a popular hangout, too. Order a pint and enjoy free popcorn while watching outdoor-themed action movies, and don't miss the Southern Appalachian Paddlesports Museum and Carolina Climbing Museum inside the store.

140 Tunnel Road
(828) 251-2001
blackdome.com

Bessemer City

CENTRAL DRUG

After the short but strenuous hike to the top of Crowders Mountain, treat yourself to a chocolate milkshake or a cherry-lemon Sun Drop at this nearby pharmacy, soda fountain, and ice cream shop — a staple in downtown Bessemer City since 1927.

112 West Virginia Avenue
(704) 629-2163
centraldrugbessemer.com

Boone

COYOTE KITCHEN

This restaurant is located at the end of the Boone Greenway. Try the "Southwest-Caribbean soul food" before or after exploring almost four miles of trails, or walk to and from the restaurant starting at the Casey Lane or Watauga High School trailheads for a mid-hike pit stop.

200 Southgate Drive
(828) 265-4041
coyotekitchen.com

Bryson City

RIVER'S END RESTAURANT

This restaurant at the Nantahala Outdoor Center started in 1972 as a simple outpost for hikers on the Appalachian Trail. Today, kayakers, whitewater rafters, anglers, and day hikers enjoy River's End's waterfront views, too, as they fill up on "Sherpa rice" or attempt to finish the one-pound Hungry Hiker burger.

13077 U.S. Highway 19
(828) 488-7172
noc.com/places/restaurants/rivers-end-restaurant

Uwharrie Mercantile

OPPOSITE: TIM ROBISON; THIS PAGE: DHANRAJ EMANUEL

Cashiers

WHITESIDE BREWING CO.

The namesake mountain in Whiteside Brewing Co.'s logo rises just beyond the brewpub's doors. Enjoy an IPA or amber ale on the lawn, or order takeout from a menu of paninis, burgers, and nachos for a picnic on top of Whiteside Mountain's 750-foot cliffs.

128 NC Highway 107
(828) 743-6000
whitesidebrewing.com

Kill Devil Hills

FOOD DUDES KITCHEN

With Jockey's Ridge State Park, Nags Head Woods Preserve, Run Hill State Natural Area, and the Wright Brothers National Memorial all within a four-mile radius, adventure is never far from this Caribbean- and Mexican-inspired restaurant. The laid-back atmosphere draws hikers, surfers, and beachgoers for fish tacos, jerk chicken wraps, and homemade desserts.

1216 South Virginia Dare Trail
(252) 441-7994
fooddudeskitchen.com

Raleigh

SUNNY'S DINER

Before venturing out to the 5,600-acre William B. Umstead State Park's lakes and trails just half a mile away, fill up on eggs, bacon, and pancakes at this traditional diner. Prefer to work up an appetite first? Sunny's serves breakfast all day long.

8710 Glenwood Avenue, No. 104
(919) 787-7715

Troy

UWHARRIE MERCANTILE

In downtown Troy in Uwharrie National Forest, a former 1909 hotel and drugstore now serves coffee, sandwiches, and baked goods to help fuel a day on the trails. Plus, peruse the pages of a book filled with handwritten memories of locals who recall the shop's past lives.

401 North Main Street
(910) 572-1555
uwharriemercantile.com

— Katie King

A GUIDE TO NORTH CAROLINA'S 41 STATE PARKS

North Carolina's first state park, Mount Mitchell, offers the same spectacular views today as it did in 1916.

PHOTOGRAPH BY CHIP HENDERSON

CAROLINA BEACH STATE PARK

CAROLINA BEACH // This coastal park is home to the Venus flytrap, a carnivorous plant unique to the wetlands of the Carolinas. Located along the Cape Fear River, this secluded area is no less dynamic than the nearby Atlantic.

(910) 458-8206
ncparks.gov/carolina-beach-state-park

CARVERS CREEK STATE PARK

SPRING LAKE // A historic Rockefeller family vacation home is set among the longleaf pines of this park, whose scenic landscape spans more than 4,000 acres, rich with natural and historical beauty.

(910) 436-4681
ncparks.gov/carvers-creek-state-park

CHIMNEY ROCK STATE PARK

CHIMNEY ROCK // Protruding from the mountainous landscape, Chimney Rock is aptly named for its geologic form. And while this granite feature is the main attraction, waterfalls and a wealth of flora and fauna are captivating, too.

(828) 625-1823
chimneyrockpark.com

CLIFFS OF THE NEUSE STATE PARK

SEVEN SPRINGS // Over time, erosion has carved out these 90-foot cliffs that loom above the Neuse River. This land was once occupied by Tuscarora and Saponi tribes, who used the river for travel and the surrounding land as ceremonial grounds and gathering places.

(919) 778-6234
ncparks.gov/cliffs-of-the-neuse-state-park

CROWDERS MOUNTAIN STATE PARK

KINGS MOUNTAIN // When drilling and excavation in nearby areas threatened the beloved Crowders Mountain, local residents convened to protect it, and this state park was established in 1973.

(704) 853-5375
ncparks.gov/crowders-mountain-state-park

DISMAL SWAMP STATE PARK

SOUTH MILLS // Once a site of extensive logging, this now-protected land has rebounded. Sixteen miles of trails lead visitors around this hauntingly beautiful landscape, and a 2,000-foot boardwalk ventures into the Great Dismal Swamp itself.

(252) 771-6593
ncparks.gov/dismal-swamp-state-park

ELK KNOB STATE PARK

TODD // Elk Knob is the only park in the state that offers cross-country skiing during the winter. Dramatic elevation changes create an endurance challenge rewarded by beautiful forests and summit views.

(828) 297-7261
ncparks.gov/elk-knob-state-park

ENO RIVER STATE PARK

DURHAM // The Eno River is tucked away amid the bustle of Durham and Orange counties, and curves along nearly 30 miles of trails. This Piedmont gem is also home to a historic mill site.

(919) 383-1686
ncparks.gov/eno-river-state-park

FALLS LAKE STATE RECREATION AREA

WAKE FOREST // Initially created to control flooding and act as a reservoir for surrounding communities, Falls Lake quickly became a popular spot for outdoor fun. Today, the Mountains-to-Sea Trail weaves in and out of the area, attracting hikers and leisurely walkers.

(919) 676-1027
ncparks.gov/falls-lake-state-recreation-area

FORT FISHER STATE RECREATION AREA

KURE BEACH // Catch a glimpse of Loggerhead sea turtles on the protected portions of the area's oceanfront, or explore the trails that weave through the salt marsh.

(910) 458-5798
ncparks.gov/fort-fisher-state-recreation-area

FORT MACON STATE PARK

ATLANTIC BEACH // Step into Fort Macon's casemates and immerse yourself in Civil War history. Or venture over to the undisturbed shoreline for a peaceful swim.

(252) 726-3775
ncparks.gov/fort-macon-state-park

GOOSE CREEK STATE PARK

WASHINGTON // Live oaks draped with Spanish moss frame the trails of this park, located in an area once home to the Tuscarora Indians, royal governors, and, later, subsistence farmers.

(252) 923-2191
ncparks.gov/goose-creek-state-park

GORGES STATE PARK

SAPPHIRE // This rugged landscape was long used for industrial purposes, until conservation efforts began in the late 1970s. Subsequent years of land donation and protection led to the creation of the park, which is now a haven for many rare species.

(828) 966-9099
ncparks.gov/gorges-state-park

GRANDFATHER MOUNTAIN STATE PARK

BANNER ELK // Home to more than 70 rare and endangered species, Grandfather Mountain has long attracted global attention for its distinctive ecology and physical grandeur. Severe weather, cliff-climbing ladders, and intense terrain make for a uniquely challenging experience.

(828) 963-9522
grandfather.com

HAMMOCKS BEACH STATE PARK

SWANSBORO // Accessible only by boat, this undeveloped barrier island was first recognized as a valuable spot by Native Americans. Dugout canoes, pirate ships, and World War II Coast Guardsmen have all prowled the surrounding shallow waters. Nowadays, visitors can still explore paddling trails and enjoy nature, undisturbed.

(910) 326-4881
ncparks.gov/hammocks-beach-state-park

HANGING ROCK STATE PARK

DANBURY // This park's namesake rock juts out from the earth like the bow of a large ship, overlooking the wooded lands below. The park is set among the Sauratown Mountains, known as the "mountains away from the mountains" for their distance from the Blue Ridge.

(336) 593-8480
ncparks.gov/hanging-rock-state-park

HAW RIVER STATE PARK

BROWNS SUMMIT // This park is a serene getaway for the Triad region, set along the Haw River with miles of trails for exploring. A boardwalk to the river stretches from the Piedmont Loop Trail, a scenic and short hike through the park.

(336) 342-6163
ncparks.gov/haw-river-state-park

JOCKEY'S RIDGE STATE PARK

NAGS HEAD // The steep, sandy slope of this dune may inspire an urge to tumble all the way down. Many do just that, or opt to hang glide, a more graceful approach to the East Coast's tallest sand dune. Roanoke Sound meets the park on its inland side, where paddling, sunbathing, and sandy shoreline trails encourage visitors to relax.

(252) 441-7132
ncparks.gov/jockeys-ridge-state-park

JONES LAKE STATE PARK

ELIZABETHTOWN // The Southeastern United States is home to around 500,000 bays, best described as slight topographical depressions in the Coastal Plains. Jones Lake is one of these features that still contain shallow open water, which invites reptiles, birds, and vegetation to settle in permanently.

(910) 588-4550
ncparks.gov/jones-lake-state-park

JORDAN LAKE STATE RECREATION AREA

APEX // B. Everett Jordan Lake proves itself to be a generous resource for both practical and recreational use. Surrounding communities rely on this 14,000-acre reservoir for its water supply and a host of fun activities on and off the water.

(919) 362-0586
ncparks.gov/jordan-lake-state-recreation-area

Lake Waccamaw State Park

KERR LAKE STATE RECREATION AREA

HENDERSON // This 50,000-acre reservoir, located along the Virginia state line, is known to Virginians as Buggs Island Lake, after an early settler of the area.

(252) 438-7791
ncparks.gov/kerr-lake-state-recreation-area

LAKE JAMES STATE PARK

NEBO // Set at the base of the Blue Ridge Mountains, Lake James has been a hydroelectric power source for Duke Energy since the early 1900s. Fittingly, it was named after the company's cofounder, James B. Duke.

(828) 584-7728
ncparks.gov/lake-james-state-park

LAKE NORMAN STATE PARK

TROUTMAN // In addition to North Carolina's largest man-made lake, this state park also boasts one of the region's most popular mountain biking networks.

(704) 528-6350
ncparks.gov/lake-norman-state-park

LAKE WACCAMAW STATE PARK

LAKE WACCAMAW // This Carolina bay is home to at least five species on the state's rare plant list, along with some aquatic species you won't find anywhere else in the world. A boardwalk trail extends 375 feet into the lake, perfect for taking in the natural surroundings.

(910) 646-4748
ncparks.gov/lake-waccamaw-state-park

LUMBER RIVER STATE PARK

ORRUM // True to its name, Lumber River was an 18th-century hotspot for timber harvest and transport. Many communities cropped up along the riverbanks as a result, some of which are still around. The park is now sectioned into three parts: scenic, recreational, and natural, all varying in public accessibility.

(910) 628-4564
ncparks.gov/lumber-river-state-park

OPPOSITE: CHIP HENDERSON; THIS PAGE: BAXTER MILLER & RYAN STANCIL

Medoc Mountain State Park

MAYO RIVER STATE PARK

MAYODAN // Smooth rocks pepper the Mayo River, where falls and flowing waters have rounded the river's edges over time. Look for well-preserved Native American fish traps, as well as leftover relics from local textile mills.

(336) 427-2530
ncparks.gov/mayo-river-state-park

MEDOC MOUNTAIN STATE PARK

HOLLISTER // Standing just 325 feet above sea level, Medoc Mountain is what remains of a mighty mountain range formed during the Paleozoic Era. Years of withstanding the elements has softened its peak, but up-close exploration reveals still-rugged terrain and steep slopes.

(252) 586-6588
ncparks.gov/medoc-mountain-state-park

MERCHANTS MILLPOND STATE PARK

GATESVILLE // A certain eerie beauty is cast upon this swamp-like environment, where bald cypress trees create winding paths for both turtles and kayaks. The primarily aquatic environment is home to many species of flora and fauna, including two primitive fish species: the longnose gar and the bowfin.

(252) 357-1191
ncparks.gov/merchants-mill-pond-state-park

MORROW MOUNTAIN STATE PARK

ALBEMARLE // The four major peaks within this park — Morrow, Sugarloaf, Hattaway, and Fall — are all less than 1,000 feet tall. Morrow Mountain has the highest elevation within the park, rising 936 feet.

(704) 982-4402
ncparks.gov/morrow-mountain-state-park

MOUNT JEFFERSON STATE NATURAL AREA

WEST JEFFERSON // This mountain, covered in a variety of wildflowers, trees, and shrubs, was once named Panther Mountain, inspired by a local legend. Later, it was renamed in honor of Thomas Jefferson and his father, Peter, who owned and surveyed nearby lands.

(336) 246-9653
ncparks.gov/mount-jefferson-state-natural-area

MOUNT MITCHELL STATE PARK

BURNSVILLE // The strenuous six-mile hike to the summit of Mount Mitchell, the highest point east of the Mississippi River, rewards those who brave it with spectacular views.

(828) 675-4611
ncparks.gov/mount-mitchell-state-park

NEW RIVER STATE PARK

LAUREL SPRINGS // This park encompasses a scenic portion of the New River, which was named a National Wild and Scenic River in 1976. Despite its name, the New River is thought to be one of the oldest rivers in North America, predating the mountains it now winds through.

(336) 982-2587
ncparks.gov/new-river-state-park

OCCONEECHEE MOUNTAIN STATE NATURAL AREA

HILLSBOROUGH // Keep an eye out for the Brown Elfin, a rare species of butterfly, while strolling this area's wooded trail. Due to this species' seasonal presence, researchers believe that the habitats of Occoneechee Mountain have remained largely unchanged since the last Ice Age.

(919) 383-1686
ncparks.gov/occoneechee-mountain-state-natural-area

Singletary Lake State Park

PETTIGREW STATE PARK

CRESWELL // This park encompasses Lake Phelps, an ecologically and archaeologically fascinating site that has witnessed thousands of years of human history. Artifacts like dugout canoes, found sunken in the lake's shallow water, provide insight into the past.

(252) 797-4475
ncparks.gov/pettigrew-state-park

PILOT MOUNTAIN STATE PARK

PINNACLE // The protruding knob of Pilot Mountain has long been a landmark for travelers. When the Saura Indians lived in the region, they used it as the "Great Guide" or "Pilot."

(336) 325-2355
ncparks.gov/pilot-mountain-state-park

RAVEN ROCK STATE PARK

LILLINGTON // Rising 150 feet above the Cape Fear River, the impressive Raven Rock was named for the, yes, ravens that once roosted atop it. Many other unique rocky features can be seen throughout the park, too.

(910) 893-4888
ncparks.gov/raven-rock-state-park

SINGLETARY LAKE STATE PARK

KELLY // Carolina bays are known to be shallow, and at just 11.8 feet deep, Singletary Lake, surrounded by old cypress trees, currently holds the title for the deepest bay lake in North Carolina.

(910) 669-2928
ncparks.gov/singletary-lake-state-park

SOUTH MOUNTAINS STATE PARK

CONNELLY SPRINGS // This area was once the site of a gold rush when the mineral was found at Brindle Creek in 1828. Today, there are hikers instead of miners. The park's beautiful landscape includes elevations up to 3,000 feet, as well as an impressive 80-foot waterfall.

(828) 433-4772
ncparks.gov/south-mountains-state-park

STONE MOUNTAIN STATE PARK

ROARING GAP // The center of this 14,000-acre park is Stone Mountain, a bald-faced dome. A restored mountain farm stands on the land below, welcoming visitors to delve into the lives of the area's early settlers.

(336) 957-8185
ncparks.gov/stone-mountain-state-park

WEYMOUTH WOODS SANDHILLS NATURE PRESERVE

SOUTHERN PINES // The longleaf pine forests of this area once spanned across the Southeast. Although the longleaf population has dwindled, this preserve provides a window into the landscape and ecology of the past.

(910) 692-2167
ncparks.gov/weymouth-woods-sandhills-nature-preserve

WILLIAM B. UMSTEAD STATE PARK

RALEIGH // Established in the wake of poor farming practices and the onset of the Great Depression, this land was purchased by the Resettlement Administration to create a public recreational area. Now bordered by Raleigh's bustling highways, this surprisingly serene land is a perfect way for city dwellers to get outside without going far.

(919) 571-4170
ncparks.gov/william-b-umstead-state-park

— Katie Schanze

NORTH CAROLINA'S 14 NATIONAL PARKS

One hundred things to know and see.

GUILFORD COURTHOUSE NATIONAL MILITARY PARK

1 A 1,900-man British force defeated Maj. Gen. Nathanael Greene's 4,500 Americans and Continentals at the Battle of Guilford Court House, but because the British suffered so many casualties, the U.S. eventually won the Revolutionary War.

2 Men from 17 counties joined the North Carolina militia, which totaled 800 soldiers.

3 Three current Army National Guard units are derived from American units that participated in the Battle of Guilford Court House.

Maj. Gen. Nathanael Greene was nicknamed "The Fighting Quaker." A monument to him stands at Guilford Courthouse National Military Park.

4 Two of North Carolina's three signers of the Declaration of Independence — William Hooper and John Penn — are buried at the park.

5 One of the 28 monuments in the park pays tribute to Kerenhappuch Norman Turner, who is said to have ridden on horseback from her home in Maryland to Guilford Court House to nurse her wounded son back to health.

2332 New Garden Road, Greensboro, NC 27410, (336) 288-1776, nps.gov/guco

PHOTOGRAPHY BY TOMMY WHITE, MARK CASKIE, ©ISTOCKPHOTO.COM/WWING

These aren't molehills, but the Great Smoky Mountains, visible from the Oconaluftee Overlook near Clingmans Dome.

MOORES CREEK NATIONAL BATTLEFIELD

6 Slippin' and a-slidin': Tallow was the key to this pivotal battle in American independence. Before the arrival of the 800 Loyalists, the 1,000-strong Patriot troops removed the planks from the bridge that crossed Moores Creek. They smeared the remaining crossing beams with tallow. As the Loyalists crossed single file, the Patriots shot at them, and the enemy fell into the creek.

7 They weren't too slick, though: It has been said that the Loyalists greased themselves, cut their hair, and shaved their beards so that the enemy couldn't hold onto them in battle.

8 Old Mother Covington wasn't anyone's mom. She was a 2½-pound cannon, and her "daughter" was a half-pound swivel gun.

9 The Loyalists were armed only with broadswords, so named because of their width. The weapons were sharpened on both edges of the blade. This allowed Loyalists who liked to fight close-up to use hand-to-hand combat.

10 The spoils from the battle included 15,000 pounds sterling in money and 13 wagons, with horses.

11 BYOM: Bring your own musket. To join the Patriot militia, you were required to provide your own gun, gunpowder, clothes, food, and canteen. You also had to be at least 16 years old.

40 Patriots Hall Drive, Currie, NC 28435, (910) 283-5591, nps.gov/mocr

In the 1930s, the 60-foot Wright Brothers National Memorial was the largest monument dedicated to a living person in the United States.

WRIGHT BROTHERS NATIONAL MEMORIAL

12 The Wright Brothers National Memorial was built using 1,200 tons of North Carolina granite, 2,000 tons of gravel, 800 tons of sand, and 400 tons of cement.

13 In 1902, at their camp in Kitty Hawk, the Wright brothers sketched the design for the 1903 Flyer on brown wrapping paper. The original sketch is in the collection at the Franklin Institute in Philadelphia.

14 But did they earn frequent-flyer miles? In 1902, the Wright brothers made 250 glides in just two days, and 1,000 glides in one month at Kitty Hawk.

15 The wheels beneath their wings: The Wright brothers financed their five years of experiments with $1,000 — that's $27,000 in today's money. The funds came from their bicycle repair shop in Dayton, Ohio.

16 And the sand beneath their wheels: The Wright brothers originally designed their famous 1903 Flyer with skids instead of wheels because the plane would have become mired in the soft sand at Kitty Hawk otherwise. It wasn't until 1910 that the Wrights installed wheels on a flyer.

17 He almost forgot to trigger the shutter, but John Daniels, who worked at the Kill Devil Hills Life Saving Station, took the famous photograph of the Wright brothers' first flight.

18 Fly me to the moon: In 1969, when Neil Armstrong took his first steps on the lunar surface, he carried with him a piece of cloth and wood from the original 1903 Flyer.

1000 North Croatan Highway, Kill Devil Hills, NC 27948, (252) 473-2111, nps.gov/wrbr

THIS PAGE: EMILY CHAPLIN AND CHRIS COUNCIL; OPPOSITE: SCOTT HOTALING

GREAT SMOKY MOUNTAINS NATIONAL PARK

19 The Smokies are estimated to be 200 million to 300 million years old.

20 They're watching you: There are about two black bears per square mile in the park.

21 More than 17,000 species of plants and animals have been identified in the Great Smoky Mountains National Park, but scientists believe an additional 30,000 to 80,000 species might live there.

22 The fog that hangs over the Smokies is the result of the 85 inches of rain — more than seven feet — that falls on the highest peaks each year.

23 Watch your step: The Smokies are home to lungless salamanders, which breathe through their skin and mouth tissue, and are also famous for their ability to regrow their limbs.

(865) 436-1200, nps.gov/grsm

At 6,643 feet, Clingmans Dome is the highest point in Great Smoky Mountains National Park.

Lean in: Love curvy roads? Ride the Blue Ridge Parkway near Maggie Valley.

24 Some hikes along the parkway are consistently popular: You may have seen the albums on Facebook of stunning fall colors (and corny poses) at the top of the Rough Ridge trail near Grandfather Mountain. But try taking the trails less traveled for surprise adventures. The Heintooga Ridge Road at Milepost 458.2, just 11 miles from the south end of the parkway, leads to Balsam Mountain, perfect for high-elevation bird-watching.

25 Although you'd be hard-pressed to find a spot on the parkway that's not picture-perfect, snapping a photo (or 20) along the magnificent Linn Cove Viaduct should be at the top of your to-do list.

26 Calm your road rage tendencies. For the entirety of the 469-mile parkway, the speed limit never exceeds 45 miles per hour, and is often much lower.

27 The shiny, heart-shaped leaves of the galax plant have been gathered in the southern Appalachian Mountains for floral arrangements and medicinal uses for generations. Now, it is illegal to do so within the park.

28 The Blue Ridge Parkway has more than twice the combined number of visitors as Yellowstone, Yosemite, and the Grand Canyon.

29 Beavers are among the most important creatures of the parkway. Thanks to their dam-building skills, which have led to an increase in bogs and wetlands, biodiversity has flourished.

30 Superstitious about holding your breath in tunnels? You might want to start training. Twenty-five of the 26 tunnels on the parkway are in North

THIS PAGE: EMILY CHAPLIN & CHRIS COUNCIL; OPPOSITE: J. CARLEE ADAMS/ALAMY

Carolina, and they make up 36 percent of the total tunnels in the National Park Service.

31 Construction of the Blue Ridge Parkway began in 1935. People serving in the Civilian Conservation Corps worked on roadside plantings and improved nearby fields and forests. The entire project, including the last seven miles near Grandfather Mountain, took more than 52 years.

(828) 298-0398, nps.gov/blri

TRAIL OF TEARS NATIONAL HISTORIC TRAIL

32 Between 1838 and 1839, nearly 4,000 of 15,000 Cherokees died on the journey to present-day Oklahoma, but some escaped the forced relocation. The Cherokees had treaty rights, and along with escaped fugitives, they formed what is now the Eastern Band of Cherokee Indians in North Carolina.

33 The Cherokees' tribal lands encompass more than 56,000 acres in five North Carolina counties.

34 In 1830, gold was found on Cherokee land. Lotteries were held to give land to the Cherokees and gold to white settlers.

35 Fort Butler, located in the town of Murphy, was one of the last internment camps for Cherokees before they were forced to travel to "Indian Territory" in present-day Oklahoma.

36 One of the stops along the historic trail is the Junaluska Memorial and Museum in Robbinsville. The museum is located at the burial site of Cherokee warrior Junaluska, who was forcibly moved from his home to Indian Territory in 1838.

37 Ralph Waldo Emerson wrote a letter in 1838 to President Martin Van Buren in defense of the Cherokee Indians.

(505) 988-6098, nps.gov/trte

The 10-acre Elizabethan Gardens are managed by The Garden Club of North Carolina.

FORT RALEIGH NATIONAL HISTORIC SITE

38 Preservation efforts began at the site in 1896, but locals were calling it Fort Raleigh and marking it on maps long before any archaeological evidence confirmed it was the settlement site of the first English colony.

39 The Waterside Theatre on the property is home to the outdoor drama *The Lost Colony*, which re-creates interactions between the English and Native Americans in the 1580s. The play was first performed in 1937, when it hosted a kind-of-a-big-deal guest: President Franklin D. Roosevelt.

40 A few hundred years after the first English colony disappeared into thin air, the site was home to another group. In 1863, free African-Americans created the Freedman's Colony. It operated only for a few years, but it was a tremendous success and home to 3,900 residents from across the South.

41 Spoiler alert for visitors expecting to see a walled village: The site consists of an "earthwork." It most closely resembles a large ditch, with high earthen walls surrounding it, which likely served as the foundation for a wooden building.

42 The earthwork on the site is now commonly thought by experts to be part of a defensive outpost, which would have guarded the fort itself. Remains of the settlement have never been found.

43 Elizabethan Gardens on the property were created to look like the kind of gardens a wealthy English colonist might have had in the 1500s. Among the many flowers in the garden is a rosebush sent by Queen Elizabeth II, from the royal rose garden at Windsor Castle.

44 It's estimated that one live oak tree in the gardens was here even in 1585, when the colonists first arrived. Unfortunately, it probably won't talk to you like the willow in *Pocahontas* did, but it's still pretty impressive.

1500 Fort Raleigh Road, Manteo, NC 27954, (252) 473-2111, nps.gov/fora

PHOTOGRAPHY BY EMILY CHAPLIN & CHRIS COUNCIL

CAPE HATTERAS NATIONAL SEASHORE

45 One theory says that the "Banker" ponies of Ocracoke descended from those left by shipwrecked explorers, who, in the 16th or 17th century, tossed the horses overboard to lighten the ship's load. In the 1950s, the Ocracoke Boy Scouts took care of the ponies, and had the only mounted troop in the nation. The Ocracoke ponies are now permanently contained and cared for on the island.

46 No, you can't go dune sledding. Federal law protects sea oats, one of the primary dune-building grasses. They can't be broken, pulled up, dug up, or damaged.

47 Landlubbers are sometimes unprepared for swimming in the ocean. Our best advice? Despite a perfect blue-skied day, you could get caught in a rip current — the opposite of a good time on vacation. Heed the weather service's daily warnings and condition reports.

48 Still a fairly rare sight, many species of seals use North Carolina beaches as a pit stop in their travels during the fall, winter, and spring.

49 Keep an eye out for gators. But what's higher in number and more likely to bite you? Mosquitoes. Seriously. Bring bug spray.

50 If you're looking for more reassurance than the old "more likely to be struck by lightning" adage, let us be the first to tell you that you're far more likely to get a blistering sunburn than to be attacked by a shark.

51 Bird-watchers, unite! More than 360 bird species call the seashore home. It's a part of the Atlantic Flyway, a globally important bird area that stretches from the Caribbean to Canada.

52 Don't mind the large, bearded guy. The infamous pirate Blackbeard, a k a Edward Teach, finally met his end in an area of Ocracoke Inlet now called Teach's Hole. Some claim to have seen a strange light glowing just beneath the water in the cove at night.

53 Sometimes the beaches glow and sparkle at night. When you kick the sand, you disturb tiny bioluminescent plankton. This creates a chemical reaction that causes the sand to glow with a blue-green light.

54 Most years, from mid-April through mid-October, the Cape Hatteras Lighthouse and the Bodie Island Lighthouse are open for self-guided climbs. Pro tip: Cape Hatteras's lighthouse is 257 steps from ground to balcony — equivalent to a 12-story building — and Bodie Island's is 200. Don't wear high heels.

(252) 473-2111, nps.gov/caha

55 You won't find vampires in Transylvania County, but you might get wet looking for them. Known as "The Land of Waterfalls" — it has at least 250 —it's also the wettest county in the state, receiving 90 inches of rain annually.

56 Thomas Edison once sent mineralogist William Hidden to find platinum in the Linville Caverns. Hidden didn't find any, but he and his guides carved their names into a limestone wall in the caves. Don't do this.

57 Before computer-generated imagery was in vogue, the train wreck scene from the movie *The Fugitive* was staged and filmed on the Great Smoky Mountains Railroad near Dillsboro. The wreckage can be found there today, Harrison Ford and Tommy Lee Jones not included.

58 Feeling fishy? The Blue Ridge Heritage Area is famous for its trout production.

59 The mountains of North Carolina are home to more species of salamanders than any other place in the world.

60 The rugged and beautiful terrain of Linville Gorge, the "Grand Canyon of North Carolina," has been known to cost more than a few hikers a ride out of the gorge in a helicopter.

61 The Fraser firs grown on Christmas tree farms in western North Carolina are called the "Cadillacs" of Christmas trees. The firs produced here account for more than 20 percent of all Christmas trees grown in the United States.

62 The Pisgah National Forest, near Brevard, is considered the "Cradle of Forestry." Dr. Carl Schenck, George Vanderbilt's chief forester for Biltmore Estate, founded the Biltmore Forest School, the first school of forestry in the nation, in 1898.

63 Two-thirds of North Carolina's apples are grown in Hendersonville in the Blue Ridge Mountains. Forget your local supermarket in favor of that roadside stand — your pies will thank you.

64 Companion plants — corn, beans, and squash — make up "the three sisters," the mainstays of the Cherokee Indians' diet for thousands of years in this area. These agricultural staples are still cultivated today. Pass some this way, please.

nps.gov/blrn

Eastatoe Falls is on private property near Rosman, but the public can visit.

THIS PAGE: TOMMY WHITE; OPPOSITE: CHARLES HARRIS

The Flat Rock Estate known as Connemara was home to Pulitzer Prize-winning poet Carl Sandburg.

CARL SANDBURG HOME NATIONAL HISTORIC SITE

65 You think your hobby is cool? Sandburg's wife, Lillian "Paula" Sandburg, raised champion dairy goats. Today, descendants of three of her prize-winning breeds are still raised on-site by Connemara Farms. The Nubian goats are the most popular with visitors, because of their floppy ears and outsize personalities.

66 To name the goats, volunteers often turn to a baby-naming book for ideas. They've also been known to draw inspiration from pop culture: see goats Tina and Turner.

67 The 40 invasive exotic plant species at the Carl Sandburg Home are there due in part to birds, and, ahem, their healthy digestive systems.

68 The Museum Preservation Center in the park is home to 325,298 of Sandburg's personal letters, telegrams, maps, photos, and movies, and a staggering 12,000 books. As if you didn't feel guilty enough about your neglected "To Read" pile.

69 If you know Sandburg's poem "Zinnia Sonata," it probably won't surprise you to learn that the family grew this annual flower. For more evidence, look to the flower beds of zinnias that line the front yard.

70 A landscaping focal point of the Sandburg Home, the boxwood shrubs that line the driveway were planted in 1850. Old age has taken its toll, but they're still standing thanks to a little extra TLC.

71 There are several rock formations in the park, including the globally rare southern Appalachian low-elevation granite domes. These outcroppings are how the town of Flat Rock got its name.

72 Each year, the site holds a poetry contest for students in kindergarten through the 12th grade.

1800 Little River Road, Flat Rock, NC 28731, (828) 693-4178, nps.gov/carl

To save your feet, replace your shoes every 500 miles. That means you'll need four pairs to hike the entire trail.

73 There are more than 250 trail shelters on the AT, generally placed five to 15 miles apart — and occasionally 30 miles, when there's a town or lodging along the way.

74 The length of the trail has often changed due to repairs, detours, and more. In 2001, it was 2,168.1 miles long. Ten years later? 2,181. Today, it's 2,193.1 miles from beginning to end. Start hiking before it gets any longer.

75 It takes about five million adult steps to hike the entire trail between Maine and Georgia. That's about one-ninety-sixth of the distance to the moon, so hiking the AT practically makes you an astronaut. Right?

76 Trail magic: unexpected acts of kindness or generosity on the trail. It can be a fellow hiker giving you a candy bar or a local handing out homemade cookies in a town along the trail. Trail angels: the people who supply the magic.

77 In 2018, seasoned ultra-marathoner Karel Sabbe thru-hiked the AT in a record 41 days, traveling an average of 53 miles per day, to become the fastest AT hiker ever. The trail usually takes around six months to complete. Um, yeah, you go on, we'll catch up later.

78 It's probably best just to stick to this useful hiking advice: The most dangerous part of the trail is the place where you are right now. The safest? Wherever you were a moment ago.

79 A common mistake hikers make is taking more gear than they need. Number one on the list of things you won't need? Books. They're heavy, take up room, and you'll be so tired, you'll fall asleep before page 2.

80 You can become a citizen scientist with the National Park Service by collecting data on flowering plants and migration patterns as

THIS PAGE: EMILY CHAPLIN; OPPOSITE: NATIONAL PARK PLANNER, WWW.NPPLAN.COM

they differ from place to place and year to year — a branch of science known as phenology. Through the AT Seasons program, you can help track 17 plant species, four birds, two frogs, and even a caterpillar. You can even use your smartphone: *appalachiantrail.org*.

81 Signature white trail blazes have been used to mark the trail since its completion in 1937. There are an estimated 165,000 blazes marking trees and posts along the AT. A double blaze is placed before turns, junctions, or other areas that require hikers to be especially alert.

(304) 535-6278, nps.gov/appa

OVERMOUNTAIN VICTORY NATIONAL HISTORIC TRAIL

82 Three weeks on foot, or, today, five hours by car: The 330-mile trail stretches over four states — North Carolina, South Carolina, Tennessee, and Virginia — and retraces the journey of American Revolutionary War militiamen to the Battle of Kings Mountain in South Carolina.

83 It rained almost the entire time, from September 24, when the first troops left Abingdon, Virginia, until they reached South Carolina.

84 With about the same number of people who attend today's Elkin High School, the 350-member Surry County Militia departed Elkin on September 27, 1780. Troops passed through Wilkesboro, Morganton, and Rutherfordton before joining other forces at Kings Mountain.

85 It took up to 15 seconds to load a flintlock musket, a common weapon in the Revolutionary War — but it felt much longer.

86 Try climbing it while carrying muskets: The trail's highest point is Roan Mountain, at 6,285 feet.

87 Grab a fife and a mountain bike: There are 60 miles of public trails along the route, including those near Lake James and Kerr Scott Reservoir.

88 Audie Rogers of Candler donated a 200-year-old South Appalachian hunting horn for use in a 1975 march that commemorated the Patriots' journey. President Gerald Ford was scheduled to attend the celebration, but because of recent assassination attempts, sent his vice president, Nelson Rockefeller, instead.

(864) 936-3477, nps.gov/ovvi

89 Every seven to 10 years, the Cape Lookout Lighthouse has to be repainted because it gets "sandblasted" during heavy winds and storms, which strips the paint. That's one way to exfoliate.

90 The National Park Service most frequently receives "rescue" calls from visitors who have walked down the beach without realizing how far they've gone and are then too tired to make the return trip. Folks often try to walk around the cape, not realizing how big the area is. Unless you're Karel Sabbe (see Appalachian Trail), we don't recommend attempting this.

91 The maritime forest on South Core Banks isn't a natural occurrence like the ones on Harkers Island. Boy Scouts planted the trees in the 1950s and '60s.

92 More than 100 wild horses live on Shackleford Banks. They used to be rounded up once a year to help control the population on the island, but since the late 1990s, that practice has stopped, thanks to pony birth control, administered by park rangers.

93 Line your pockets with the right kind of dollars — sand dollars. Brown and fuzzy means the creature is still alive — hands off — while white and smooth means the shell is yours to take.

94 There may not be lifeguards on these remote islands, but there *are* rules. Visitors are limited to taking home a maximum of two gallons of shells per day.

PHOTOGRAPH BY GORDON CAMPBELL/ATALTITUDEGALLERY.COM

Take a three-mile boat ride to the remote Cape Lookout National Seashore.

Harkers Island Visitor Center
1800 Island Road
Harkers Island, NC 28531

Beaufort Visitor Center
701 Front Street
Beaufort, NC 28516

(252) 728-2250
nps.gov/calo

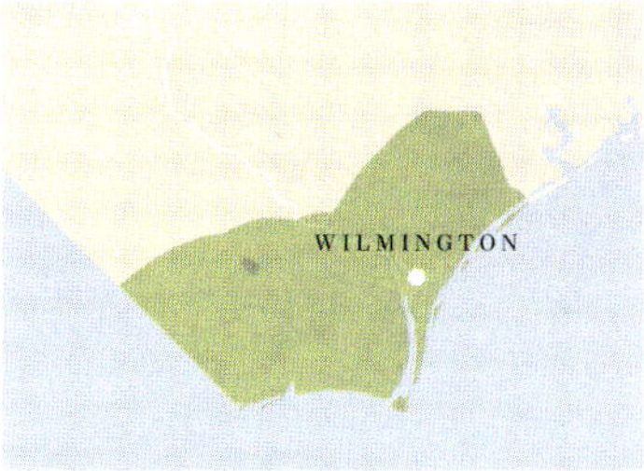

GULLAH/GEECHEE CULTURAL HERITAGE CORRIDOR

95 Longer than North Carolina, the 546-mile corridor is one of the newest national heritage sites, running from Pender County through South Carolina, Georgia, and to Duval County, Florida.

96 Gullah/Geechee communities were formed by West African slaves who wanted to create their own traditions in the Low Country of South Carolina. Their folk tales, music, art, and cuisine have become integral to their native — and American — heritage.

97 North and South Carolina are home to the Gullah culture, while Georgia and Florida are home to the Geechee culture. The Gullah and Geechee communities share similar linguistic and cultural traits, which have remained intact through several centuries because of the relative isolation of the region.

98 Language bound the communities together: The Gullah/Geechee people developed a separate Creole language — the only African-American Creole language in the United States. With elements of English and more than 31 African languages, it contains more than 3,800 words.

99 Weight lifters and brothers CJ and Omar Cummings from the Gullah/Geechee Nation set new records and won gold medals at the 2013 Youth Pan American Games.

100 *American Idol* winner Candice Glover is a Geechee descendant.

(843) 818-4587, nps.gov/guge

— Ellis Dyson & Katie Schanze

TO ORDER MORE

If you've enjoyed *North Carolina Outdoors*, think of your family members, friends, and coworkers who would enjoy it, too!

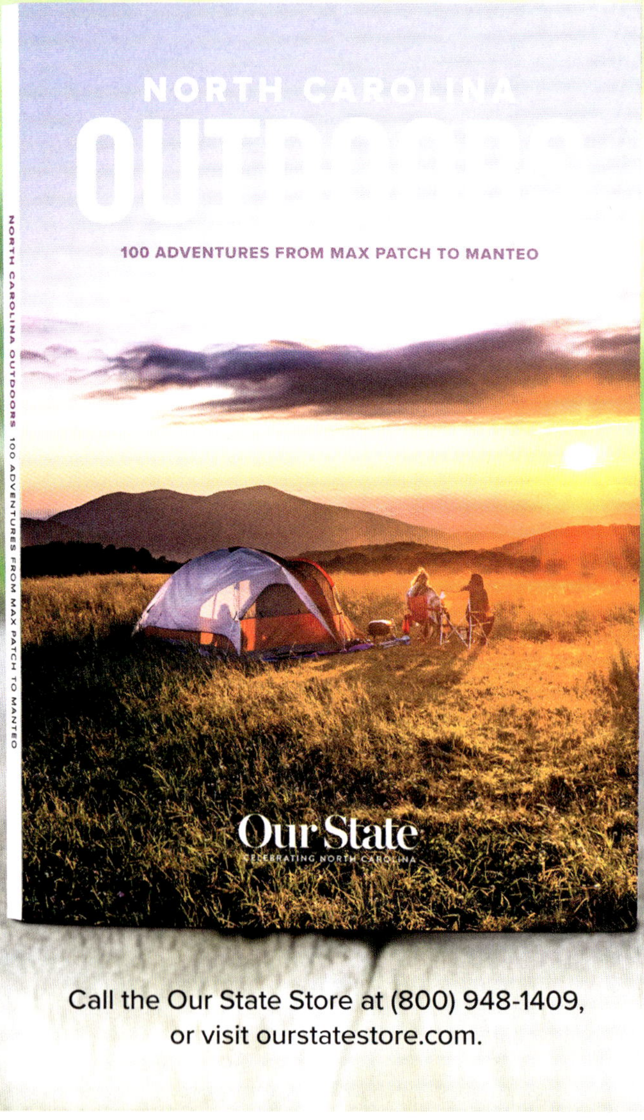

Call the Our State Store at (800) 948-1409, or visit ourstatestore.com.